THE SOKODAE:
A WEST
AFRICAN DANCE

I0165096

Drid Williams

1971

MONOGRAPH SERIES NO. 7

The Institute for Cultural Research

About the Author

DRID WILLIAMS was a professional dancer for thirty years before becoming a social anthropologist. She completed graduate degrees from St. Hugh's College, Oxford, in 1976. She has recently completed a book for the University of Illinois Press entitled *Anthropology and The Dance: Ten Lectures* (Urbana-Champaign, 2004). She has done fieldwork among Carmelite nuns, Dominican friars and the Royal Ballet Company in England and among Aboriginal communities in Northern Queensland. She has taught at Moi University in Kenya; at the University of Sydney, Australia; and New York and Indiana Universities in the United

States. She is founder of the *Journal for the Anthropological Study of Human Movement* (JASHM), first published in 1980, and she is the architect of a theory of human actions called semasiology.

NOTE

This monograph is based on the text of a lecture delivered under the aegis of the Institute for Cultural Research. Original material collected during 3½ years' study in Ghana.

The Sokodae:
A West African
Dance

THE COMPLEXITY, richness and diversity
of today's world, plus an unprecedented
fund of available information in every
field of human endeavour, produces
fascinating areas of study, particularly
in the social and behavioural sciences.
The study of Dance, one very small
and specialised facet of potential
research in social anthropology, has
unique attractions, advantages and
disadvantages. Some of the latter
are connected with the fact that in
Western societies, 'the dance' has been

DRID WILLIAMS

classified not as an object of research but primarily as entertainment or as a means towards aesthetic enjoyment. These classifications, of course, have not always reflected the attitudes of specialists. Over forty years ago, Prof E.E. Evans-Pritchard pointed out that

> In ethnological accounts the dance is usually given a place quite unworthy of its social importance. It is often viewed as an independent activity and is described without reference to its contextual setting in native life. Such treatment leaves out many problems as to the composition and organisation of the dance and hides from view its sociological function.[1]

In so doing, he indicated a core of

2

concern for future research in the dance field, specifically about '...problems as to the composition and organisation of the dance...' which, sufficiently unravelled, can yield insights not only into the sociological function of dance but into its nature and meaning as a system of non-verbal communication and conceptualisation as well.

Material from my own recent work in Ghana which took place over a period of three and a half years and which seems to be of interest to specialists and laymen alike could be summed up, for the purposes of this discussion, in these two often repeated questions about dance research:

(1) *What* does one study: movements, 'emotional expression' or what? (2) *Why* does anyone study this sort of thing at all?

This paper will use materials

presented in the lecture given for the Institute for Cultural Research on October 31, 1970, and some additional notes, suitable for a written exposition of the lecture. It will deal principally with some of the answers to the first question, outlining components of the composition and organisation of a dance (in this case, Sokodae) which begin to form a rough outline of the general structure and relationships involved in the unit being studied, and to the extent which space permits, we will also examine a partial answer to the second question: *why* does one undertake such a study?

When people ask that kind of question, I often wish that they would formulate the query in somewhat plainer terms, terms which would, I think, state what is really on their minds; that is, of what *use* is the study of an African dance to anyone in a highly organised, technological society? The Sokodae, the dance around which this whole discussion turns, is a dance which belongs to the Ntwumuru people, a small group of approximately nine thousand human beings, who live in the north-eastern section of central Ghana. They are part of a larger group of Gang-speaking peoples, including the Rachis, whose history and present society is intimately involved with this dance. Are these people and this dance not completely remote from our interests?

Not as much as we might think. Study of Sokodae, and of many other African dances, can be of use to us simply *because* they are from different environments, different traditions and different atmospheres. This may seem a rather obvious point, but it is one which in my opinion can hardly be stressed too much, because we are, from a perspective of these differences, rather ill-equipped to judge or to criticise these dances or to try to do anything, at the outset, except understand them. It has been my experience that many people are willing to try to understand, even if the process involves some loss of cherished notions and/or stereotypes, but it is at this very point, no matter how positive an attitude we may have or how sympathetic we try to be, that we are in difficulties about which we are frequently unaware. These difficulties lie in our habits of thought, some of our culturally conditioned, basically learned ways of seeing and responding, which can actively prevent, or at least obstruct, our understanding traditional African art forms in the ways their practitioners understand and practise them, or, for that matter, the traditional arts of India or Islam as well.

For example, many people (as I am sure my readers are all aware) look at an African mask and they either say or think to themselves, 'That was made before these people understood anything about perspective or anatomical drawing.' In a like manner, many people look at an African dance (or think about it) as a rather disordered and chaotic affair. If not that, they think that it is a totally improvised, spontaneous and 'free' expression which lacks form of any kind, and this is because, first of all, they are used to seeing dance with a picture frame around it – this built-in picture frame in Western minds in relation to dance is a proscenium stage opening. Second, they seem to want to believe that at least in the dances of Africa they might find some untrammelled, uninhibited 'expression' of human beings, an attitude which involves two stereotypes: (1) that of the emotionally and sexually uninhibited African and (2) that of the naive belief that all dance behaviour is somehow 'symptomatic' of the participants' feelings. Thus, they are in danger of conceiving of these dances as being the first simple, if not childish and undisciplined beginnings in what they imagine is a 'world history' of the dance, which culminates in classical ballet or in some other contemporary Western theatrical dance form.

This point of view is, to be quite blunt about it, just dead wrong, for it assumes that these people are (or were) trying to do the same things with their art that we try to do. It assumes that their art has the same reasons for existing that ours does and that they (poor dears!) just missed the point somehow. Dance research, or research into any of the traditional art forms of the world, can demonstrate beyond any doubt that other societies are (and were) not trying to do the same things with their arts that we have done with ours, at least for the last two hundred years, and that their criteria for what we call 'art' was (and is) quite different from ours. Moreover, these kinds of attitudes are appallingly ethnocentric and condescending.

Four of the major differences in criteria reflected in the Sokodae dance are these:

(1) The Ntwumuru and Krachi peoples, like the people of most pre-industrialised societies, are not expressing *themselves* in their dances so much as they are *expressing a set of ideas* which are

meaningful to them. The truth of this assertion should become apparent when, later on, we examine the oral tradition for the Sokodae dance and the seven sections of it. This lack of the Western concept of 'personality' or 'individuality' means that –

(2) Their art is not an end in itself; it is a means towards an end. It is not a 'product' in the same way that art is a product within the context of industrialised, producer-consumer societies, which means that –

(3) We must not forget that all of this kind of art is anonymous, as was most of the art in the Western world before the Renaissance. Neo-African art, including the dance, has acquired many of the same conventions as present day Western art together with 'personality cults'. These phenomena seem

to be inevitably associated with industrialisation, and finally –

(4) Traditional African art is not relevant (in the plastic and graphic areas) because it is 'like' Picasso or Modigliani or, in the dance field, because it is 'like' the works of Pearl Primus, Alvin Ailey or Martha Graham or any other contemporary dancer. Nor is it relevant primarily because of its design, composition, or aesthetic surfaces, elegant and beautiful though they may be.

This art is relevant because of its content, because of the functions which it performs on the societies in which it exists and it is considered to be 'successful' in traditional terms if it 'works', that is, if it accomplishes the purpose for which it is done.

We must therefore try to understand the Sokodae (or any other traditional art form) in terms of *its* content and *its* criteria; an attempt which is much more akin to an anthropological rather than a Western aesthetician's view of art in general – a view which in our contemporary world hardly needs an apology. Most anthropologists are committed to trying to understand how people outside of their own cultures think; they are committed to trying to understand the contents and meanings of cultural behaviour in any society, including their own. They tend to bring the same kinds of attitudes to bear upon dance, ritual and art forms which are a vital and ubiquitous group of social phenomena in West Africa.

The results of this anthropological commitment in reference to art are myriad, but for our purposes, two points are perhaps most important: research of this kind can produce fresh, interesting points of departure for a re-evaluation of both the products of art and of artistic behaviour in our own society and it also means that in the next section of this paper, I shall attempt to tell you what the dance, Sokodae, is *about* in contrast to telling you 'about the dance', for in finding out what Sokodae is about, I believe we will get nearer the mark.

Ee---eee---eeee---
Akyemba, agyanka bedi agoro,
Agoro, agoro
Agoro a eye me de nono
Agoro
Eee---ee---Akyemba, agyanka
Agoro, agoro.

Ee---ee---eeee---[2]
The weaver bird's child, the orphan, comes to dance, Dance, dance

This is the dance belonging to me
(which I own) Dance.
The child of the weaver bird, the
orphan, comes to
Dance, dance.

This song, in the Twi language with
its English translation, is one of the ones
sung in the first section of the Sokodae
dance. It is reproduced here because it
contains the three key ideas which the
Sokodae is about: (1) Ownership, (2)
Orphan and (3) Birds in general and
the weaver bird in particular.

In order to establish their ownership
of the dance and to give some idea of its
age, the Ntwumurus tell the following
story from their oral tradition.[3] In
1750–1800, the Ntwumurus crossed
the Volta River (see map at end of
article) from the western to the eastern
side with the intention of settling in the

new location. They had to abandon their homes on the western side of the river because of infringement by the Juabens. Some of the Ntwumuru clans sought the protection of Dente[4] in the Krachi area and some of the kings of the Ntwumuru and the Basa fled to the Republic of Dahoumey where they settled at Safe, Gbede. The Bejamso Ntwumurus did not go to Dahoumey, but to the place where they established the present village which bears their name.

It was through conquest, therefore, that the chief of the Twi-speaking Juabens (called the Juabenhene) became the overlord of these areas and over many of the other Guang peoples as well.[5] The Krachis, for example, had already crossed the Volta some time before and were permanently settled in their present area south of the Ntwumurus. They simply submitted without any warfare to the Juabenhene's rule. Dente became more and more important to the Juabens, who appropriated all of the customs and traditions related to Dente because their own Obosom (gods) did not have the power of prophecy, of seeing into the future. Dente did.

When the Krachis, Ntwumurus and other peoples belonging to the Guang group became subjects of the Juabenhene, they had to pay homage to the Juaben chief. These annual homage payments took place at the Juaben festivals of Apafram, a yearly affair which the Ashantehene holds for the whole Ashanti State, of which the Juabens are a part. At this time, the Krachis and all of the subservient peoples presented gifts of slaves, sheep, elephant tusks, fresh fish, meat, honey and salt to the Juabenhene. Besides this, the Ntwumurus of Bejamso came to honour the Juabenhene with the drumming and dancing of the Sokodae. Usually, the Krachis and Ntwumurus, after paying tribute, would go back to their homes across the river.

One year, they were not granted permission by the Juabenhene to return to their homes. They were kept at the town and they were used to labour on the farms of the Juaben chief and his elders. The visitors resented this imposition very much but they were afraid to act. They were sorely outnumbered and, of course, completely unarmed. The result of this was that they stayed for some time before they finally decided to ask for the help of Dente in their plight. They invoked the powers of Dente by calling his special names and by playing the drums and horns of the Sokodae.

The story emphasises that Dente reacted to these appeals of his troubled people very strongly, for several things began to happen to the Juabens; heavy storms destroyed part of the town, elephants destroyed crops and many of the townspeople were caught and mangled or killed by leopards and lions. The Juabenhene consulted many oracles to try to find out what was behind all of the trouble.

The oracles told him that he was keeping the Krachi and Ntwumuru people in Juaben against their wills and more important, against the will of Dente. The Juabenhene was ordered by Dente to let his people return to their homes across the river.

Not wishing any further ills and misfortunes to fall upon his people and lands, the Juabenhene ordered that the former prisoners should go. He sent special messengers along with them who were accompanied by slaves in order to ensure that Dente would know of his obedience to his wishes. The slaves were given as gifts to Dente, who subsequently ordered them to be distributed among several nearby villages.

It is interesting to know that after this, the Juaben chief sent his drummers and dancers who were adept at the Kete (an Ashanti dance done only for chiefs) to dance in honour of Dente in Krachi. The Krachis didn't want these visitors to be in Krachikrom (the capital of the Krachi State) proper, so they assigned them a place to stay which was near to the old Krachikrom, now inundated by the waters of the Volta Lake. People used to say, 'I am going to where they are playing Kete.' Gradually, this developed into 'I am going to Kete-Krachi', the two words which make up the present name of Ketekrachi.

It is in this way that the Sokodae is intimately connected with the known oral history of the Ntwumuru people. We are told that the dance was already done many years before this event took place. The fact that the Ntwumurus had this connection with a Twi-speaking people for so long accounts for the fact that some sounds like the weaver bird's song referred to earlier were translated into Twi from Ntwumuru. The song quoted was especially important, because the Ntwumurus wanted to be sure that the Juabens clearly understood the origins, meaning and ownership of the dance.

The other two ideas connected with the weaver bird's song are somewhat different both in character and in kind;

the notion of 'orphan' and that of 'birds'. Orphan has no literal meaning as we would understand it as it is used here; the dance is not about someone who has lost his or her parents. It has what we might call a figurative meaning stemming from the fact that that Sokodae dance belongs to everyone. This dance has no 'parents'; that is, it is not restricted in any way to persons of a particular cult or class. It does not require any special knowledge nor does it have any priests attached to it. All Ntwumuru may participate in it regardless of status, economic standing or other considerations.

Another kind of ownership of this dance is expressed in connection with ideas about birds: that part of the song which says, ' ... which belongs to me' or 'which I own'. The 'I' is used in a generic sense; it means I as Ntwumuru. The idea is expressed symbolically through associations with the weaver bird. As everyone knows, this bird builds one of the most complex and distinctive nests to be found among the feathered species. No other bird can reproduce it. The Ntwumurus see themselves as the weaver birds and the Sokodae as the nest. May I hasten to point out here that by no means is there any confusion in their minds as to whether they are really weaver birds or not, any more than there is any confusion in an English ballet dancer's mind as to whether she is really a swan while performing Swan Lake. The weaver bird in Sokodae is used in a conceptual fashion, as we shall see.

The major motif of the Sokodae is that of the courting and mating of birds. In the first section of the dance, which is called Kowurobenye (Kowurobe =

orphan, nye = has got it), the men dance in clockwise and counter-clockwise circles simultaneously. They present a striking spectacle with their brilliantly coloured cloths streaming out behind them. The cloths in motion extend the male dancers' bodies like the bright tail plumage of peacocks, cockatoos and parrots. The movements all suggest the bowing, strutting and ecstatic rushing movements of the courting male bird. Our informants pointed out to us that in the Kowurobenye, the males rival each other for the attention of the females. Within the step patterns, they even try to bump against one another in an attempt to knock each other off balance so that they will make their rivals appear clumsy and unaccomplished to the audience of watching women.

The second section of the dance is

a female counterpart of the first male section, although the movements are quite different. Men, if they wish, can change the positioning of their cloths to simulate how women wear them and dance in this section as well. In decided contrast to the strong locomotor movements in the first section, the movements in this section, called Kenemoe, are subtle and delicate both in terms of footwork and movements of the torso. The whole of the torso is involved in a kind of light rippling movement from front to back having no lateral overtones at all. Sometimes, this move is carried into the head and neck, reminding one of fowls walking or pecking softly at grains of food. The word, Kenemoe, means a movement, which makes it a little difficult to translate!

The third section of Sokodae called

Kumumuwuru (spinning) is probably the most spectacular from a Western point of view. It involves whirling, spinning turns done by the men in solo sequences. They practice the rather difficult manipulation of their cloths privately – part of the physical skill required to do the step properly – for the cloth must be made to rise up in such a way that the upper part of the body is invisible. While turning, the total shape of the man and his cloth should resemble a tulip blossom and stem. The men do this to 'make themselves look beautiful' – and it does. Kumumuwuru is done for the same reason that the peacock spreads his tail or vibrates in the sunlight, making his beautifully coloured wings bedazzle the female.

The two women will usually dance the fourth section, which is another women's section, together. The kind of step involved in this section makes a track in the earth and the way the footwork is accented is closely related to the name of the section; Kikyen, pronounced roughly 'key-chen', with the accent on the last syllable. This step makes a track in the earth, and the evenness of the steps and the straightness of the track are desired results of the performance of the step. It is interesting to know that this type of step may be observed in many parts of Ghana, always in women's dances and usually in dances involving puberty and marriage. There seems to be a strong association between women and the earth among the Ntwumurus and throughout Ghana. The essential meaning of this step is that it is important that a woman makes her mark firmly in the earth, for it symbolises her passage through life.

THE SOKODAE: A WEST AFRICAN DANCE

The fifth section of Sokodae is danced
by men and women together. The
name, Kedenkenkyew, is taken from
the drum beats. This whole passage of
the dance is freely, strongly and boldly
erotic. Contrary to uninformed and
ill-informed opinion, this is one of the
comparatively few dances or pieces of
dance among many hundreds in Ghana
which has the theme of eroticism as its
content. The movement patterns are
quite consistent with the overall theme
of courting and mating birds already
established in previous passages
of the Sokodae. Kendenkenkyew's
movements are unselfconscious, direct
and unmistakable in their meaning.
The atmosphere is one of heightened
awareness, joy and ease; a genuine
zest for living seems to pervade the
whole dancing community. There is
a complete absence, of fear, hatred,

shame or frustration – a total contrast to much of what currently passes for eroticism on the Western theatre dance stage.

Kyenkyenbrika, 'step-step-turn around', is the sixth section of Sokodae and it is also danced by both men and women. They do not necessarily dance together, however, as in the previous section. If someone wishes to dance solo, they may do so. One of the most interesting gestures for women occurs chiefly in this section. The woman points to her forehead with her right hand and to the small of her back with her left. This means that the woman follows the man with her mind and supports him with the strength of her back. The image given by our informants to explain this was that 'all during the day from the morning the woman follows the man in her mind when he is hunting or in the fields. At night, when he comes home, he rests and she tends to his needs, feeding him and serving him – all this because of the strength of her back.' Women use this characteristic gesture whether dancing alone or with men.

The concluding section of Sokodae, Kedenkyenkprofe, also a name taken from the drums, contains the greatest variety of step patterns. It is danced mainly by men, with the women occasionally forming complementary patterns, either with the Kikyen or the Kenemoe steps. There is one gesture which means, 'I am a true son of the land', another which means that the dancer's great grandfather killed a man in battle. A complex series of jumps, changing from one leg to another means, 'My father was an Ojya', which means a priest of one of the state gods.

We were told that in the old days,

only older men would dance Sokodae
with cloths. All cloth was handwoven
then and younger men would not have
acquired sufficient wealth or status
to have them. The young men wore
waistbands and a loin-cloth and danced
with their arms lifted to simulate
the outspread wings and breast of a
courting male bird. Now, everyone
wears an imported Java-print cloth, or
a cotton cloth made in Ghana or an
Adinkira[6] cloth. The art of weaving
has, to my knowledge, disappeared
among the Ntwumurus.

The musical ensemble which
accompanies Sokodae is of special
interest. It includes both drums and tusk
or head horns. There are six drums in all:
the master drums, Kitinmpene, which
are pitched 'talking' drums, supported
by one Kakwedji and two Prentren, all
accompanied by a 'dondo', the familiar

'squeeze drum' of West Africa. The tusk horns, called Ntahera in Twi are seven in number.[7] They are led by the master horn, named Kabretense, which plays melodies somewhat reminiscent of plainsong. Accompanying this horn are two Kajesolo, two Namu and two Brekye. A gong accompanies the horns, for they are often played by themselves with no drum accompaniment. Originally, there were three of each type of horn, totalling twelve horns in all. It is not known why there are only seven horns in use now. These horns are now made from the head horns of the buffalo, but in the past were made from elephant tusks.

Once a year, the drummers, horn-players and a group of dancers come to Ketekrachi from Bejamso to dance the complete Sokodae to honour Dente, thereby taking active part in the

Dente festival. This annual observance commemorates the occasion upon which Dente freed his people from the Juabens. One of the results of this is that parts of the Sokodae, Kowurobenye and Kumumuwuru, are done in the Krachi area and have come to be known as the 'Krachi Flying Dance'.

The Sokodae dance is considered to be 'in the hands of the chief' who can command it for special occasions for the gods or whenever else he chooses. It is performed upon special funeral occasions; for example, when the present Asafohene[8] of Bejamso dies, this dance will be drummed and danced for seven days. Once a year, Sokodae is danced and played for Sonko, one of the traditional war gods of the Ntwumurus. Sonko's shrine is situated outside Bejamso in the bush and it is visited by most of the people during April. Great amounts of guinea corn are provided for the ceremonies, prepared three days in advance by the old women of Bejamso into 'pito', a kind of fermented wine. Six or eight male goats are obtained as sacrifices for Sonko. On the eve of the ceremony, the Sokodae is danced. There is a contest between the two divisions of the town, Lentae and Chambae, in clearing the path to the shrine. It is a time of high celebration. These kinds of occasions and any others which are of great import are the occasions which belong to Sokodae.

The dance, one of the ancient art forms of Man, if not the oldest of them all, has many sources, many impulses and many uses. Considered only superficially, we are confronted in Sokodae merely with a group of adult people who are imitating the

DRID WILLIAMS

movements of birds and we may well ask why do people do this sort of thing. Is this not a childish, simplistic, if pretty and pleasurable activity?

I think not, for it seems that in an attempt to classify, categorise and explain their impressions, in attempts to formulate in non-verbal symbolic terms their knowledge about their particular universe, men have used the movements, colours, shapes and sounds derived from other creatures and from nature to convey their ideas about the nature of the phenomenal world. In the case of the Sokodae, the weaver bird (or rather, selected characteristics about it) has been used to communicate ideas about various social relationships and divisions of labour between men and women. This propensity to conceptualise in these kinds of ways is, according to Lévi-

Strauss,[9] one of the most fundamental characteristics of the human mind.

We might reflect profitably on the fact that although a dance like Swan Lake concerns some rather fundamental notions about psychological transformations, instead of social roles or divisions of labour, groups of adult Western dancers have for the last century been imitating the movements of swans. By this statement, I do not mean to imply that Swan Lake and Sokodae are *the same* in terms of form, neuro-muscular coordination systems involved, idiomatic gestures, costumes, etc. but I do mean to say that *on a certain level of conceptualisation*, the use of weaver birds and swans as vehicles for whole constellations of ideas about the nature of Man, is in fact similar. At this point I feel constrained to add, because of the intellectual level of this particular audience, that neither Swan Lake nor Sokodae reflect the highest levels, either of conceptualisation or of function which it is possible to attain through the dance. This is a fact which is abundantly clear even through reading available extant literature about various forms of dance in the Near and Far East, but this in no way lessens the importance of dances of the same genre as Sokodae and Swan Lake within the context of their societies and I hope that even this brief examination of Sokodae has contributed to an enlargement of understanding of the phenomenon of 'a dance'.

The forms of Sokodae undoubtedly arose from such fundamental urges towards coherence as Lévi-Strauss describes and were consistent with the direct perceptual experiences of the Ntwumuru people. The content, meaning and symbolism attached to these forms, as we have seen, represents an attempt to order experience into intelligibility through a kind of reasoning by analogy. It is also apparent that Sokodae is the living expression of the social identity of at least nine thousand people. The dance offers many insights into human relationships and behaviour, relationships which are important to the Ntwumurus themselves.

Dances, regardless of where they are found in the world, are highly organised, highly structured human symbolic behaviour. They reflect, as it is possible to see even from the one example of the Sokodae, an interesting and fairly broad range of ideas, associations, cultural mores, value systems and symbols belonging to the societies in which they are embedded.

Monica Wilson[10] has said:

> Ritual reveals values at their deepest level... men express in ritual what moves them most, and since the form of expression is conventualized and obligatory, it is the values of the group that are revealed. I see in the study of rituals the key to an understanding of the essential constitution of human societies.

Our remaining problem in this discussion pertains also to the first of the questions stated at the beginning of this paper, '*What* does one study?' From the previous section, we see that much of the data collected pertains to the oral traditions surrounding the dance, the musical accompaniment, costume and other material culture and specific postures and gestures, but all of this should not be collected in a random fashion by any means.

In dance research, one must first take into consideration and then account for at least six components of the unit being studied, which fall into two related space-time groupings: (1) the physical space and (2) the physical time of the dance, (3) the social space and (4) the social time of the dance, (5) the conceptual space and (6) the mythological time of the dance. 'A dance' is, after all, a complex, self-contained finite event which takes place within the larger what we might call 'non-finite' (in relation to it) phenomenon which we call society. A dance has a beginning, a middle and an end and while each one will have a different configuration of elements within the structure outlined above, each one can be profitably studied using that structure as a plan from which one commences work. In this paper, I will only deal briefly with the spatial elements involved in a dance.

The physical space of a dance is the easiest to define; for example, the proscenium stage might be forty feet wide and twenty-five feet deep, with a nineteen-foot vertical opening, or perhaps it is larger or smaller. On the other hand, the physical space may be a forest clearing one hundred feet wide and two hundred feet long filled with people who are leaving only a comparatively small open space (or spaces) in the centre, the physical dimensions of which are marked off by an arrangement of drummers and singers and some seats for priests and priestesses. In Sokodae, the physical space was the 'square' or meeting place in the village of Bejamso, near the chief's house, partly shaded by an enormous mango tree by which the people gathered, making a circle or 'dance space' approximately forty feet in diameter. Or, the physical space of a dance might be a semi-circular arrangement of people seated upon cushions and divans on a raised platform or series of steps, with the dancer being the focal point at a place on the marble floor which is equidistant from either end of the semi-circle, if it were a performance of Kathak in the north of India. A list of examples could be extended almost indefinitely, but these should serve to give some idea of what is meant by the physical space of a dance.

The component of physical space which had just been described is actually the 'contextual' space of a dance. There

is a second and equally important
component of the physical space of a
dance which I call the 'apparent space',
i.e. the measurable distances which the
dancer, or dancers, travel during the
dance. These may vary enormously.
In much Western theatrical dance,
for example, the distances travelled
are often quite large, as in a series of
jumps or turns which is extended over
a line twenty or thirty feet long. On
the other hand, these distances may be
comparatively small, as in the case of
Kathak or Bharata Natyum, where the
dancer rarely moves more than three to
five feet in any given direction from the
starting point of the dance. Sokodae has
great variation among its sections in
the apparent spaces used in the dance.
They were quite long in the Kikyen
section where the women were making
a track in the earth, and relatively short

where the couples are confronting each other in a section like Kedenkenkyew, the erotic section. If anything could be called an 'aesthetic surface' of a dance, it is this configuration of what I have called the apparent physical space.

The social spaces and social distances in a dance are not so easy to define, but one key to the understanding of these concepts may be found in works with which this audience is familiar, that is, *The Silent Language* and *The Hidden Dimension* and *The Territorial Imperative*[11] although these works do not confine themselves to dance, but deal with the subject of social spaces and distances in a much more general way. In Sokodae, the social spaces involved are reflected in the fact that in some sections of the dance, only men dance and in others, only women, and in some, both. Dances are very often about *social* roles and as a consequence, reflect the distances between various roles and how the actor can function within the social space of any given role. We might safely speculate that all human social roles have, sometime, somewhere, been included in dance: hunters, warriors, kings, mothers, princesses – the lot.

A second very important component to the whole notion of social space is that of the social meanings given by the particular society to such fundamental spatial oppositions as right/left, up/down, forward/back and inside/outside. This is a rather vast subject on its own, and I can do no more than suggest it here. In my lecture, however, I demonstrated some of the more fundamental of these, emphasising the right/left opposition in greetings and in other ceremonial contexts. All societies have their own customs which are assigned meanings in reference to these oppositions, and I have included at least one good reference for further reading.[12]

The idea of the conceptual space of a dance can, in this paper, receive little more exhaustive treatment, but for an excellent clue as to the meanings of this level of understanding a dance, I can do no better than to suggest Keith Critchlow's excellent book,[13] especially the drawings and explanation about the conceptual space which is behind the Laban system of dance movement and notation and which is based upon a truncated icosahedron. The conceptual space of the ballet is based upon an octahedron, as are some of the contemporary forms of theatrical dance. All of the Ghanaian dance which I studied has as its conceptual space a half-hemispherical kind of form with inclined planes radiating into the centre of it. The whole concept of balance is different in the Ghanaian dances from that of either Western or Indian forms – at least the two I have previously mentioned. Ghanaian dance is not based upon an axial notion of balance, as I also tried to demonstrate in my lecture.

We might conclude from this, then, that studying 'a dance' is a little bit like studying buildings or bridges. The first level involves the actual 'skyscraper', its bricks, stairs, lifts, decorations, etc. The second brings us to the notion of the super-structure, the steel grid framework, which although not seen by our eyes, holds the building up. The third level of knowledge about a skyscraper includes the pattern of tensile and stress forces, weights, cantilevers, etc. which are expressed in the form of blueprints. Finally, we arrive at the notion of the idea in the architect's mind, which includes that level of conceptualisation which Lévi-Strauss tries to discover; that factor in (or of) the human mind which has produced skyscrapers, igloos, huts and temples. Some might argue that this is carrying the notion of the human agency and human ego a bit far, as Western scholarship is seemingly wont to do; however, that is a subject outside the scope of this paper. Suffice it to say that Lévi-Strauss has performed a service for anthropology in that his ideas have introduced a confrontation in academic circles of the whole question of human subjectivity in relation to some rather old-fashioned mechanistic and deterministic models of Man.[14]

Or we might conclude that a study of bridges is incomplete unless it involves at least three levels: physical bridges, social bridges and mythological bridges. Similarly, the study of 'a dance' is incomplete if it does not include at least as a start the physically apparent dance, the social meanings involved and the conceptual and mythological aspects of it. Given these elements as a start, we might eventually arrive at some clear notion of what 'a dance' is.

SHADING INDICATES NTWUMURU TERRITORY

NOTES AND REFERENCES

1   Evans-Pritchard, E.E. *The Dance (Azande)*. Africa, vol. 1, no.4, October 1928, p.446.

2   The orthography of the Twi language uses phonetic symbols which are not possible in this publication, therefore the following signs have been used as substitutions and the approximate English pronunciations are given:

o is the sound 'awe' in English e is the sound 'eh' as in 'bet'.

Ky always has the sound of 'ch' as in 'church' N at the beginning of a word like Ntwumuru is pronounced, not 'en,' but like it's sound N-N-N. In this particular word, the 'tw' has the sound 'ch' as well. N has the sound of 'ng' in 'sing'.

3   The Krachis, Yejis and Ntwumurus all tell this story and they are all quite positive about it. It would seem that it is to some extent 'historically valid' in a Western sense, because the event it recounts marked the beginning of the

independence of the Krachi State as it
exists today; that is, it's independence
from Juaben domination, not from the
nation of Ghana. This story also agrees
with accounts from the Ashanti-Juaben
history according to Dr. Adu-Boahene,
Dept. of History, Legon. There are
obvious mythological elements in the
story as well, so that the whole tale might
best be characterised as a mythological
charter for the dance. Malinowski ('Myth
in Primitive Psychology', *Magic, Science
and Religion*, 1948, Glencoe, Illinois),
although many of his ideas are old-
fashioned in social anthropology today,
nevertheless stressed the importance of
myth as a *charter*, thereby focussing upon
the living relationship of myth to society,
and removing somewhat such stigmas
from the notion of myth as those of
'falsified history' or 'phantasy'. Whether
or not the story is 'true' or 'false' history
from an European point of view, however,
is really irrelevant. The fact that the story
has a role in connection with the dance

and the fact that it *validates* the position and function of the dance in present day Krachi and Ntwumuru society is both more important and is what is relevant about it.

4 Dente: noun, also Lente, also Konkom, although this latter name is never used in speaking. Dente is the highest of the Ikisi (gods) of the Krachi, except for Nana Brukun, who is older. The Krachis brought Dente with them to their present location when they moved from there during the 19th century. Dente resides in a cave a short distance from Krachikrom. When the capital had to be moved to a different location (where it is shown on the map) because of the flooding of the Volta Lake, Dente moved as well and took up his abode in another cave about a mile or so from Ketekrachi.

5 Krachis and Ntwumurus, together with Nkonyas, Gonjas, Nawures, Atwodes, Anums, Kyrepongs, Efutus and Yejis form the large linguistic group known as the Guang (also spelled Guan) people. Guang

means 'run-aways' in Twi.

6   Adinkira (or Adinkra) is a name given to cloth which is hand-block-printed with very old symbolic patterns, usually black on a brilliant coloured cloth.

7   There is some controversy over the original ownership of these horns; some people claim they were originally Akan, actually Ashanti, horns which the Ntwumurus copied. A set of Ntahera are even now used as 'state horns' by the Ashantehene. They are carved elephant tusks. However, these horns themselves, according to the Ntwumurus, were originally owned by an Ntwumuru chief, Atere Firam. Evidence to support this claim, hence original Ntwumuru ownership, is to be found in *The Ashanti Court Records*: In the Asantehene's 'A' Court, Kumasi, in the matter of Kumawuhene vs. Dwanhene, 1951, pp. 53, 55, 59, 61 and 75. The Ntwumuru chief, Atere Firam, lost a war to the Ashantis, and the horns were a part of the 'Dwira' (booty) that the Ashantis took from him.

8 'Asafo', noun, Fanti language. Means roughly 'body', 'group' or 'company'. The French word 'corps' is a better translation. An Asafohene is simply a leader of a group.

9 Lévi-Strauss, Claude. *La Pensée sauvage*. Paris Plon, 1962. (Author's note: it is well to remember that although the English edition of this book bears the title, *The Savage Mind*, the French word 'sauvage' has none of the connotations which the English word bears; it simply means untamed.)

10 Wilson, Monica. 'Nyakusa Ritual and Symbolism'. Reprinted in *Myth and Cosmos* edit. by J. Middleton, The Natural History Press, N.Y. 1967.

11 Hall, E.T. *The Silent Language*. Fawcett Publications, Greenwich, Conn. USA. 1959.
Hall, E. T. *The Hidden Dimension*. Bodley Head, 1966.
Ardrey, Robert. *The Territorial Imperative*. Paladin Paperback, 1967.

12 Hertz, Robert. *Death and the Right Hand*, (first pub. 1909). Trans. by Rodney and Claudia Needham. 1960,

University Press, Aberdeen.
13 Critchlow, Keith. *Order in Space*.
Thames and Hudson, 1969.
14 Claude Levi-Strauss: *The Anthropologist as Hero*, Eds. Nelson and
Tanya Hayes. M.I.T. Press. Cambridge, Mass., 1970.
(Two articles of this collection are of special interest: the ones by Bob Sholte and Peter Caws. The latter in particular is an exposition of this confrontation.)

A list of all the monographs to be published in the series:

Vico's Theory of the Causes of Historical Change
Leon Pompa, M.A., Ph.D.

Some Unusual Aspects of Communication
Edward Campbell

The Indian Guru and his Disciple
Peter L. Brent

Exploring Human Behaviour in Groups
A. John Allaway

Education and Elitism in Nazi Germany
Robert Cecil

Cultural Imperialism
Robert Cecil

The Sokodae: A West African Dance
Drid Williams

My Years with the Arabs
General Sir John Glubb

Some Effects of Music
Professor D.B. Fry

Science, Technology and the Quality of Life
Dr. Alexander King

Physiological Studies of Consciousness
Robert Ornstein

Purposes in Education
Dr F.D. Rushworth, K.R. Minogue, Sir John Wolfenden

An Eye to the Future
Dr. Alexander King, Dr. Martin Holdgate, Eugene Grebenik, Dr. Kenneth Mellanby, George McRobie

East and West, Today and Yesterday
Sir Stephen Runciman, Patrick O'Donovan, Peter Brent, Sir Roger Stevens, Nirad C. Chaudhuri, Iris Butler, Prof. G.M. Carstairs, Richard Harris

Science and the Paranormal
Leonard Lewin, D.Sc.

Sufic Traces in Georgian Literature
Katharine Vivian

Rembrandt and Angels
Michael Rubinstein

Biological and Cultural Evolution
Mary Midgley

The Age of Anxiety: a Reassessment
Malcolm Lader

Goethe's Scientific Consciousnes
Henri Bortoft

The Healing Within: Medicine, Health and Wholeness
Robin Price

A Clash of Cultures: The Malaysian Experience
David Widdicombe, Q.C.

Evaluating Spiritual and Utopian Groups *Arthur J. Deikman, M.D.*

Malta's Ancient Temples and Ruts
Rowland Parker & Michael Rubinstein

Cults in 19th Century Britain
Robert Cecil

Black Culture and Social Inequality in Colombia
Peter Wade

Urban Legends and the Japanese Tale
David Schaefer

The Role of 'Primitive' People in Identifying and
Approaching Human Problems
Contributed by Cultural Research Services

The Use of Omens, Magic and Sorcery for Power
and Hunting
Contributed by Cultural Research Services

Ritual from the Stone Age to the Present Day
Contributed by Cultural Research Services

Problem-solving and the Evolution of Human
Culture
Stephen Mithen

Cultural Identity: Solution or Problem?
Peter Wade

Inventions and Inventing: Finding Solutions to
Practical Problems
Kevin Byron

Problems, Myths and Stories
Doris Lessing

Modern Primitives: The Recurrent Ritual of
Adornment
Contributed by Cultural Research Services

The Pagan Saviours: Pagan Elements in Christian
Ritual and Doctrine
Contributed by Cultural Research Services

The Marketing of Christianity: The Evolution of
Early Christian Doctrine
Contributed by Cultural Research Services

The Press Gang: The World in Journalese
Philip Howard

Taboos: Structure and Rebellion
Lynn Holden

Paranormal Perception? A Critical Evaluation
Christopher C. French

The Unseen World: The Rise of Gods and Spirits
Contributed by Cultural Research Services

Godmakers: The First Idols
Contributed by Cultural Research Services

The Universal Ego
Alexander King

Conclusions from Controlled UFO Hoaxes
David Simpson

Jokes and Groups
Christie Davies

Creative Translation
David Pendlebury

The Crusades as Connection: Cultural transfer
during the Holy Wars
Contributed by Cultural Research Services

Baptised Sultans: The contribution of Frederick II
of Sicily in the transfer and adaptation of
Oriental ideas to the West
Contributed by Cultural Research Services

Brain Development During Adolescence and Beyond
Dr. Sarah-Jayne Blakemore

Collective Behaviour and the Physics of Society
Philip Ball

Counter-Intuition
Dr. Kevin Byron

Music, Pleasure and the Brain
Dr. Harry Witchel

Fields of the Mind
Dr. Rupert Sheldrake

Why do we leave it so late?
David Canter

Scheherazade and the global mutation of
teaching stories
Robert Irwin

Consciousness, will and responsibility
Chris Frith

Extraordinary Voyages of the Panchatantra
Ramsay Wood

www.ingramcontent.com/pod-product-compliance
Lightning Source LLC
Chambersburg PA
CBHW020606030426
42337CB00013B/1239